Benji works out in a wash tub
before moving on to the big tank
at Marineland.

Other Benji books distributed by
Scholastic Book Services:

BENJI AT WORK
BENJI (TAKES A DIVE) AT MARINELAND

Joe Camp's

BENJI

©MCMLXXVIII MULBERRY SQUARE PRODUCTIONS, INC. TM

(Takes a Dive) at Marineland

by RITA GOLDEN GELMAN

SCHOLASTIC BOOK SERVICES

New York Toronto London Auckland Sydney Tokyo

The familiar, bottle-nosed *dolphin* is often called a *porpoise* (por-pus). Sailors used to call the dolphins they saw at sea "porpoises" —and they're still called that at Florida's Marineland.

Unless otherwise credited,
photos courtesy Mulberry Square Productions

ISBN 0-590-31547-1

12 11 10 9 8 7 6 5 4 3 2 1   12   1 2 3 4 5 6/8

*To Mom and Dad
with love*

Contents

The stadium at Marineland, Florida.

What's going on?

Benji Goes for a Swim

THOUSANDS OF people push their way into the stadium at Marineland, Florida. They hurry past the flamingos, the penguins — even the piranha and the octopus. They barely glance at the dolphins, usually the main attraction. And the dolphins, darting back and forth in their pool, seem puzzled. They keep poking their sleek heads out of the water to see what—or who—is attracting such a crowd.

It's BENJI — the famous dog with the big brown eyes. Benji is at Marineland for a few weeks to film a television special; and Frank Inn, Benji's owner and trainer, has agreed to let Benji have some time off from the filming to make a personal appearance during the dolphin show. When people hear that Benji is going to be part of the show, the crowds pile in.

At last, everyone is seated in the stadium bleachers that flank the pool. There is loud, welcoming applause when Benji races across the walkway and jumps onto a floating surfboard. Then, Benji stands on his hind feet while a dolphin tows him around the pool.

Next, Benji climbs a 14-foot ladder and leaps off a platform into the pool.

Finally, toward the end of his performance, Benji has a race with a dolphin—the dolphin swims; Benji

Benji being towed by a dolphin.

runs along the pool's ledge. In the final part of the race, Benji is supposed to cross a little bridge. Just as Benji steps onto the bridge, Frank calls out, "Benji, roll over." Benji, as usual, follows instructions. But as soon as Benji begins to roll, Frank realizes that the bridge is too narrow. In rolling *over,* Benji is about to roll *off.*

But Frank and Benji are both experienced pros. Thinking and talking fast, Frank calls out, "Benji, go for a swim." At that instant, Benji rolls off the bridge, flops into the water, and paddles happily to Frank. The crowd bursts into cheers and applause. Only Frank and Benji know about the last-minute change in the program.

Benji passing the bridge where he later rolls off as if he intended to!

A Crazy Idea

BENJI AND FRANK attract crowds wherever they go. And they love to perform. But this time they were not at Marineland just to entertain their fans. They were there because Joe Camp, Benji's writer-director-producer, had come up with an idea that everyone said was crazy. Joe wanted to make a television show about a scuba-diving dog.

"You're out of your mind," everyone said. "You can't teach a dog to scuba dive. Forget it."

Once, years earlier, Joe might have listened to that kind of advice. When he first became Benji's director, he used to call Frank on the phone and ask, "Do you think you can get Benji to walk along a wall, leap across a roof, and jump through a window?" Or, "Do you think he can open a drawer?" "Can he talk on the telephone?"

Benji can do anything.

The answer was always, "Of course." After a while, Joe stopped asking. Benji could do just about anything.

And that's why Joe decided to pursue his "crazy" idea. He was going to make a movie about a dog who could scuba dive. No dog had ever done it before? Then Benji would be the first.

The Diving-Suit Problem

IN ORDER TO scuba dive, a diver needs a scuba-diving suit. And when the diver is a dog, that's a problem. You can't just walk into a sporting goods store and say, "I'd like a small bubble and a medium-sized jacket for my dog, please. He'd like to go scuba diving."

In fact, Joe couldn't even find a company that would *talk* about designing a suit for a dog. He tried. He wrote to several companies. One of them wrote back,

"The challenge you present in designing underwater equipment for a dog could be easily met; however, I am afraid you would lose the dog. . . . My advice to you is to allow Benji to do all of his underwater work free-diving. In that way, we will all have him around to enjoy for a few more years."

Another company advised Joe that they could make a suit, but it would be a waste of time and money. It was impossible to teach a dog to scuba dive. Joe kept on asking and being told, "No. It's impossible. . . ."

Then Joe met Richard Vaughan. Joe was on vacation in the West Indies. Richard was his scuba-diving teacher, and also an industrial engineer.

Joe popped up after one dive. He took out his breathing device, flipped off his mask, and turned to Richard. "Do you think you can design a scuba-diving suit for a dog?"

Instead of staring in disbelief, as others had done, Richard quietly thought about it. He had sailed around the world for seven years. He had heard and seen a lot of strange things. "Why not?" was his answer.

"Come to dinner and we'll discuss it," said Joe.

Over dinner, Richard agreed to design a suit and get it made. Joe's instructions were simple: "It has to look good and it has to work."

The Bubble

RICHARD THOUGHT a lot about the design of Benji's scuba-diving suit. He knew that Benji could not hold something in his mouth and breathe, the way most scuba divers can. Benji would need a bubble with air constantly pouring in—and out.

Richard made a sketch. That was the easy part.

Finding someone to *make* the bubble was the hard part. Big companies weren't interested in making one bubble . . . or even three. They figured there wasn't much of a market for dog bubbles.

So Richard checked out some small companies. After plenty of remarks like, "Are you crazy?" from

DESIGN FOR BUBBLE

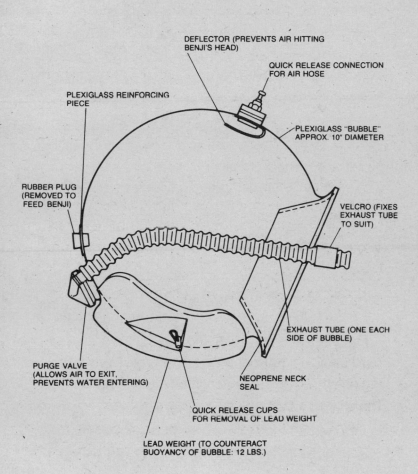

DEFLECTOR (PREVENTS AIR HITTING BENJI'S HEAD)

QUICK RELEASE CONNECTION FOR AIR HOSE

PLEXIGLASS REINFORCING PIECE

PLEXIGLASS "BUBBLE" APPROX. 10" DIAMETER

RUBBER PLUG (REMOVED TO FEED BENJI)

VELCRO (FIXES EXHAUST TUBE TO SUIT)

PURGE VALVE (ALLOWS AIR TO EXIT, PREVENTS WATER ENTERING)

EXHAUST TUBE (ONE EACH SIDE OF BUBBLE)

NEOPRENE NECK SEAL

QUICK RELEASE CUPS FOR REMOVAL OF LEAD WEIGHT

LEAD WEIGHT (TO COUNTERACT BUOYANCY OF BUBBLE: 12 LBS.)

various possible bubblemakers, Richard found Mr. Pollard, a craftsman who was proud of his work and fascinated by the project Richard proposed.

Mr. Pollard had never made a diving-bubble before, but he had been working with plastic for many years. He would make Benji's bubble by blowing up heated plastic, a little like blowing up a balloon.

Mr. Pollard built a frame out of pieces of wood. The top part of the frame had a hole in it a little bigger than Benji's neck.

The bottom part of the frame had a smaller hole.

The heated plastic went in the space between the two pieces of the frame.

Mr. Pollard's plan was to blow air through the bottom hole so that the plastic, heated in an oven beforehand, would stretch into a bubble and harden.

Making the frame had been easy. It was not so easy to blow a perfect bubble. Some of the bubbles burst. Some of them cracked. Some had lumps. Others had holes.

All together, Mr. Pollard blew about forty-five bubbles in order to get three perfect ones.

Richard took the three good bubbles to a scuba-diving company where he worked with the engineers. Together they drilled the holes, attached the hoses, and added the finishing touches. They worked slowly, precisely. Everything had to be air-tight and perfect.

Perfecting the bubble.

The Jacket

THE PURPOSE OF a scuba diver's jacket is to help the diver to float high or low in the water, whichever he or she wants. On each side of the jacket is a little pocket that blows up like a balloon. If there is a lot of air in the pockets, the diver will float near the top of the water. As the air is let out, the diver will sink. When people-divers reach the depth they want, they stop letting out the air in their jackets.

Richard knew that Benji would not be able to regulate his jacket by himself. The jacket would have to be regulated before Benji went into the water.

In designing the jacket, Richard had to be sure that Benji had plenty of room to move around . . . whether he was running or swimming. There could be no tight places that might rub his fur. Richard

DESIGN FOR JACKET

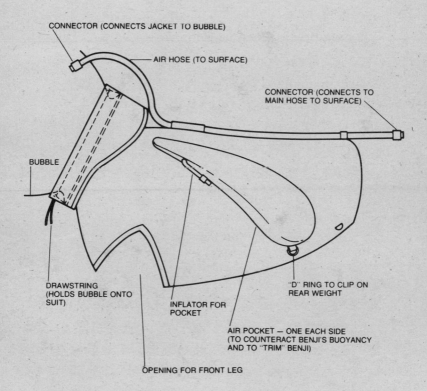

CONNECTOR (CONNECTS JACKET TO BUBBLE)

AIR HOSE (TO SURFACE)

CONNECTOR (CONNECTS TO MAIN HOSE TO SURFACE)

BUBBLE

DRAWSTRING (HOLDS BUBBLE ONTO SUIT)

INFLATOR FOR POCKET

"D" RING TO CLIP ON REAR WEIGHT

AIR POCKET — ONE EACH SIDE (TO COUNTERACT BENJI'S BUOYANCY AND TO "TRIM" BENJI)

OPENING FOR FRONT LEG

realized it was up to him to see that the jacket fit just right, because Benji wouldn't be able to tell him if something was wrong.

Benji was measured. Jackets were made and rejected. Altogether, six jackets were made; three were just right.

Just right, that is, until Benji went into the water. Everyone had forgotten that when Benji was wet, the fluff and puff of his fur flattened out and took up less space. Then the jacket became too loose. Richard refitted the jacket; and finally, Benji, Richard, and Frank were ready to teach Benji how to scuba dive.

Benji's diving suit—counting all the expenses— had cost more than $10,000.

Benji tries out the diving jacket.

Benji Learns to Wear a Bubble

BENJI, like most of us, had never worn a diving bubble. So the first step in his scuba training was to let him wear the bubble for a while and get used to the feeling.

At the bubble tryout were Frank, Richard, Frank's wife, Juanita—and of course, Benji. They had gathered in the kitchen of Frank's house. The bubble they were about to put on Benji was an oversized reject. Richard had cut some holes in it so Benji would get plenty of air.

Frank and Richard slipped Benji's head through the rubber cuff of the neck hole. The rubber would prevent water from coming in at the neck when Benji was in the pool. The rubber is similar to the elastic cuffs on a winter coat that keep the wind from blowing up your sleeves.

Benji must have wondered what was going on, but he never questioned Frank. Benji will do anything Frank tells him to do—even if it's to wear a ridiculous plastic thing over his head.

"OK, Benji. Go play with the cat."

Benji in a playful mood. He loves to play with Jackie the cat.

The dolphin is
king at Marineland.
But now there's a
new attraction!
Who is it?

It's Benji, that's who!

"I've come to dive," Benji tells newswoman Lana Afghana. (below) Now Benji notices her *for the first time.*

You expect me to do that? Benji is shocked.
(below) Oh, boy, here he comes!

My good pal Frank. (below) An actor pauses before taking the plunge.

Lana, between takes, shows that she is part sea creature. (below) Lana gets a little tired of B. W.'s endless talk.

Here I am, as ready as I'll ever be. (below)
Preparing to dive.

This is almost the real thing, except that
I'm swimming with a diver. (below) Now!
This is the life. Look, Frank, I'm a scuba diver!

Frank let go and Benji nearly toppled off the chair. The bubble weighed only ten ounces, but Benji wasn't used to it.

As Benji rounded around the corner after the cat, he forgot that he had a bubble on his head. Ping! Benji bounced off the wall. Luckily, he was wearing a protective helmet. Benji was going to have to learn to adjust his movements to his new big head.

A week later, Frank went on a fishing trip. Benji went with him. Two or three times a day, for ten or fifteen minutes, Frank put the bubble on Benji. Benji also wore a jacket reject.

During his one-month vacation, Benji became a tourist attraction in the little fishing town. He rode on the back of a Honda in his diving suit. He sat in his jacket and bubble in the boat while Frank fished. Benji went shopping in the local stores and walking by the lake in his red and yellow jacket and his big plastic hat.

Benji learned to climb steps without losing his balance, and he learned to turn corners without banging his bubble. By the time Benji and Frank returned home, Benji was very comfortable in his diving suit. And Richard was waiting with a new, smaller bubble that seemed perfect.

But Frank still wasn't ready to put Benji in the water in the diving suit. Frank wanted to test the bubble first. He had to be absolutely certain that no water would get inside.

Frank found a plastic container that had a neck just about the same size as Benji's. He put dog hair around the neck of the container and put the container into the bubble. Richard attached the air hose, and they put the whole thing in the water. The container stayed dry. The bubble worked. They were ready to go on.

Frank, Richard, and Benji test the bubble at a cage set up in Frank's backyard pool.

A Suited Benji
Goes in the Water

THE NEXT STEP was to put Benji in the water.
They started in a small wading pool.

Richard attached the air hose to the bubble, and
they put Benji in. There were no weights on the bubble, so it floated. Benji swam happily across the little
pool, paddling with his paws as though he had always swum with a bubble on his head.

The air that was blowing into Benji's bubble came
from a tank on the side of the pool. It went into the
bubble through one hose and out through another.

The "out" hose had a special valve on it that let air out but prevented water from coming in.

So far, so good. Now they had to get Benji *under* the water.

Humans and dogs naturally float in water. To pull themselves under water, they need weights. Scuba divers often wear belts made of lead weights. Richard decided that Benji's weights should be on the bubble. There were eight pounds of air pressure in the bubble that needed to be counterbalanced. Altogether, twelve pounds of weights were required to pull the twenty-one-pound Benji under.

Richard had to be careful *where* he placed the weights. If they were put on the *side* of the bubble, they would twist Benji's neck. If they were on the *top*, Benji would be turned upside down. Also, the weights had to be placed where they wouldn't hide Benji's face when the underwater camera filmed his dive. The weights had to be set under Benji's chin.

When the weights were set, Frank began Benji's underwater swimming practice — in a wading pool.

The first underwater swims were easy. Benji had no trouble breathing inside the bubble; he'd had a lot of practice. His jacket was very comfortable. And

Benji had been swimming for years. He was a terrific swimmer.

In preparation for Benji's transfer to the big pool, Frank bought an underwater microphone so that he could talk to Benji while the dog was submerged.

After several days in the two-foot wading pool, Benji was ready for deeper water.

Frank talks with Benji on the underwater mike, as Benji swims in his suit and bubble.

The Big Plunge

IMAGINE Frank's backyard. There is a swimming pool with a wooden deck on one side. Benji is standing on the platform. Richard is sitting next to him. Frank is standing in the water. Frank and Richard are dressing Benji in his suit.

The jacket is in place. So is the bubble. Richard ties a shoelace; it tightens the jacket around the collar of the bubble to make a snug fit so that no water will leak in.

Once Benji's bubble is in place and the weights are attached, someone must hold up Benji's head.

Benji's neck is not strong enough to hold the twelve pounds of weights when he is not in the water.

It takes about ten minutes to get Benji all suited up. Finally, he is ready for the plunge.

Frank lifts Benji onto a wire mesh platform that is suspended from a cable above the pool. There is an identical platform on the other side of the pool. Benji is going to swim from one platform to the other.

Richard lowers the platform — and Benji — into the water. On the underwater microphone Frank tells Benji to swim.

Benji takes off. He is two feet below the surface of the water, swimming with all four legs toward the other platform. His air hose floats on the water behind him. Richard and Frank are close by.

Benji is moving along nicely. Then, halfway across the pool, Benji stops swimming. He pulls up his front legs and puts his front paws on the ledge formed by the weights under his chin. He stops moving. Frank calls to him to swim, but Benji remains still. Frank is frightened. Something is wrong. He rushes to lift Benji out of the pool and onto the platform.

They Work Out Some Problems

ONCE BENJI IS out of the water, he seems fine. Frank removes the bubble and feeds Benji a piece of steak. Benji wags his tail.

They try again. The same thing happens. Halfway across the pool, Benji stops swimming and puts his paws on the weight ledge. Again, Frank rushes to lift him onto the platform.

Again and again, the same thing happens. Each time, Benji is carried to the platform. Each time, he seems fine.

After a while, Frank realizes what is happening. Benji is playing a game. Why swim when someone is willing to carry you and feed you pieces of steak?

It's actually quite nice down there, feet resting on the ledge, waiting to be carried.

Frank and Richard discuss the problem. They decide to change the shape of the weights so that they don't provide such a comfortable resting place.

That's where Wally comes in. Wally is an animal trainer who is assisting Frank. He volunteers to make some new weights. He melts some lead and pours it into a sand mold. Then he files the hardened lead into a new shape, one that has no place for Benji to put his feet. Wally spends hours at the work table in the yard. He ends up with two weights. They put one inside the bubble and one on the outside.

Richard and Wally work on the weight problem while Benji relaxes.

Now Benji has no place to rest his front paws. So he swims, wiggling his way from one platform to the other, all four feet paddling.

But Frank is still not happy. He is bothered by the fact that Benji is not getting his reward after each swim. Benji has always been taught that when he does a good job, he gets a reward, usually a piece of steak. But the bubble is so cumbersome to take off that Benji is not being rewarded quickly enough.

Frank asks Richard if it is possible to put a little door with hinges on the front of the bubble. That way, when Benji swims across the pool, Frank can open the door and give Benji his steak.

Richard looks at Frank and sees that he is serious. So Richard explains that a little door with hinges couldn't possibly keep out the water.

Wally finally comes up with what seems a perfect solution: drill a little hole in the bubble about the size of a nickel and cork it with a black rubber plug. While Benji swims, the plug keeps out the water. When Benji finishes his swim, he gets his steak through the feeding hole.

It works. Benji begins to swim with enthusiasm, knowing that when he gets to the other side, he'll have a piece of steak. When Frank tells Benji to

Benji receiving his reward.

swim, Benji's little body wiggles through the water like a fish. The feeding hole has made the difference.

After several days of practice, Benji finally swims a perfect lap. "Great," shouts Wally. "That was great." He pulls out the cork and gives Benji two pieces of steak. "Hey, Frank, did you see that?" calls Wally, hurriedly shoving the cork back into the hole. In his enthusiasm, he shoves his fingers right through the thin plastic. The tiny feeding hole becomes a ragged hole, five times its original size. And it's the only bubble they have on hand. The others have not yet arrived.

Training is halted while Richard patches up the bubble with another piece of plastic. And the extra bubbles, when they come, are all reinforced with an extra piece of plastic to allow for enthusiasm.

The TV Special
Takes Shape

WHILE BENJI IS in Sun Valley, California, practicing scuba diving, Joe Camp is in Dallas, Texas, working on a script for *Benji Takes a Dive at Marineland,* the television special.

When he starts out, the only thing Joe knows for sure is that the major event of the half-hour special will be Benji scuba diving. Joe wants the television show to cover Benji's amazing new skill like a news event. You know — "We are about to witness a spectacular event. Before your very eyes Benji is going to become the first dog in the world to scuba dive.''

Actually, since no one (except Benji's trainers and a few friends) has ever seen Benji dive, the TV special *will* be a news event.

Joe decides that he'd like to hire a real TV newswoman to star in the special. She could talk about the diving suit, about how Frank taught Benji to dive. And then, at the end of the half hour, with the television world looking on, she would introduce Benji's historic dive.

Joe begins looking around for a newswoman to play the part. As he is making up his list of possible newswomen, someone suggests that Joe ought to get Miss Piggy.

Joe's eyes light up. He likes the idea. The more he thinks about Miss Piggy, about putting her together with Benji, the more excited he becomes. Miss Piggy and Benji. They could talk to each other. Miss Piggy would understand Benji, and then she could translate for the television audience. Joe could write into the script a special kind of communication that could never take place between a real person and a dog.

Joe rushes to the phone and calls Miss Piggy. But her answer is no. She has other commitments. She is going to be in England making her own movie.

Joe is disappointed; but once the idea of a puppet has lodged in his head, he can't shake it out. A real person just doesn't seem right anymore. If he can't get Miss Piggy, Joe will create his own puppet-newswoman.

Joe calls an artist and they talk about possible characters for the part.

Their first idea is to find an appropriate sea creature, since the show takes place at Marineland and it's all about an underwater dive. A sea-creature newswoman. The artist makes some sketches.

Joe studies the sketches. "There's something wrong," he says. "Benji's a dog. He ought to have dogs around him. He'll relate to them better. And when this show is over, maybe they can work together again."

So the artist creates Lana Afghana — part newswoman, part dog, part sea creature.

And B. W., Benji's agent. A hard-selling, fast-talking bulldog from Texas.

The lovely Lana Afghana
talks into her mike.

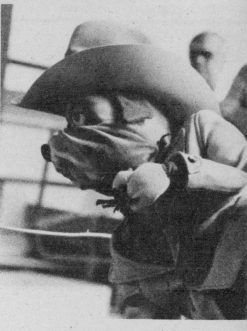

B. W., Benji's agent.

Boris Todeth, mean person.

And last, a villain. Every good story needs a villain, and Boris Todeth is mean. Boris figures that if any dog is going to be the first scuba diver, it's going to be Boris — even if that means stealing Benji's equipment and feeding Benji to the sharks.

The sketches go off to the puppet-makers. Within three weeks, Lana, B. W., and Boris are fully created. With the help of some ace puppeteers, the puppets develop voices, personalities, funny little quirks.

By the time everyone arrives at Marineland, Lana, B.W., and Boris seem as real as the people around them.

A Simple Plot

IT IS EARLY in October, sunny and warm in Florida. Cars, trucks, and vans are piling into the motel at Marineland. They are carrying the cast, the crew, the director, the equipment, and Benji, the star. The preparations are finished. Joe is ready to begin shooting the TV special, *Benji Takes a Dive at Marineland*.

The plot of the special is simple. Benji plays himself, a famous actor and well-known celebrity who is about to become the first dog in the world to scuba dive.

There is, of course, a beautiful woman, Lana Afghana, a news reporter who falls in love with Benji.

And there is a bad guy, Boris Todeth, who tries to steal Benji's scuba suit and make the dive himself. In the end, Benji makes his dramatic dive and becomes an instant hero. His feat is forever recorded by a plaque at Marineland.

There are some unique problems involved in creating this TV special. The characters are from three different worlds. There are the animals: Benji, the dolphins, other assorted marine life. There are the puppets: Lana Afghana, B. W., Boris, and a group of singers. And there are the real people: Cecil, a Marineland executive; Jesse, a singer; Richard, a sailor. Somehow, all three worlds have to come together in one show. Joe Camp and his crew are especially excited by the challenge.

Jesse Davis, a Calypso singer.

The Filming Begins

OPENING SCENE: Sailing toward Marineland on his 46-foot sailboat, *Sea Woof,* is Benji, the famous star. With him are Jesse Davis, a calypso singer (person); and Richard Vaughan, playing the part of a sailor.

As the camera rolls, Benji is standing at the rear of the boat. The wind is blowing his fur. Water is splashing his face. The boat is rocking. Benji is looking out across the ocean at the sunrise.

It is very peaceful. Nothing but Benji, his friends, and nature. A voice in the background announces:

"This . . . is Benji. And during the next half hour, history will be made as the world's most huggable hero voyages to Marineland of

The Sea Woof.

Florida and attempts to become the world's first dog to scuba dive among the beautiful and mysterious creatures of the sea. To become the only dog in history to see firsthand what many humans have never seen."

A simple scene. Less than a minute on the television screen. But on television no one will ever see the helicopter circling overhead, or Frank Inn, crowded into a corner inside the cabin of the boat.

In order to film Benji and his friends on the deck of the *Sea Woof,* the cameraman has to be in a helicopter. And in order for Benji to perform, Frank has to be nearby, but off camera.

If you could peek into the cabin while they are filming this scene, you would see Frank standing on a bed, legs spread apart, leaning against a pole. His head is twisted so that he can call directions to Benji through an open porthole. The rocking boat makes Frank's position very precarious; so, throughout the whole scene, someone has to hold Frank's legs to keep him from falling over. From where Frank is "standing" he cannot see Benji.

The script calls for Benji to walk along a ledge to the front of the boat. Frank is concerned that Benji might be blown overboard by the wind from the helicopter. With all the noise, Frank wouldn't even hear the splash.

So Frank is in touch with the helicopter by walkie-talkie.

As it turns out, Benji, as usual, doesn't miss a step. With the fierce wind from the propellers blowing against his little body, with the intense noise from the motors of the monster machine in his ears, Benji performs like the professional actor that he is.

Frank, on the other hand, gets seasick.

Lana and Benji Meet

SCENE 2: The Lovely Lana Afghana (a puppet) is about to make her first appearance in the show. The hairdresser is brushing Lana's long blond hair. "It's so windy," she tells him. "It'll never stay."

As the cameras roll, Lana speaks into a hand microphone:

LANA: Hello. I'm Lana Afghana, and I'm speaking to you from Marineland in Florida. Our cameras are here today so that you might be a part of an historic event performed by Benji, canine superstar of film and television. Benji intends to become the first dog

Lana and her hairdresser.

in the world to put on scuba gear and actually go underwater. . . . The question of the day is: why does Benji want to risk his life and limb to go where dog has never been before? We've asked his manager and confidant, B. W. Puggit, to join us in hopes of getting an answer to this question.

B. W. Puggit is long-winded. If there's a long way to say something, B.W. always picks it. He talks on and on and on. Lana becomes impatient. She tries

"Cut, cut," movie star Benji is thinking. But he waits politely for B.W. to finish his speech.

to interrupt, but B.W. won't stop talking. Finally, Lana says firmly:

"... I think Benji is the best one to tell us why he wants to make this dive ... Benji!! Could you join us for a moment?"

Up to this point, Benji and Lana have never met. Benji actually flew in from his home in Sun Valley, California, last week. Lana has only just arrived from Dallas.

Now Benji jumps between B.W. and Lana. He barks at B.W. and turns to look at Lana. Their eyes lock.

As the camera comes in for a close-up of Lana, she utters a small gasp. Somewhere in the distance, we hear the romantic rippling of a twinkling harp. Lana is dazed, stunned ... then, finally:

LANA: I had heard that you had big beautiful brown eyes, but I had no idea they were so ... so ...

Lana trails off as words fail her.

Lana sees Benji's big brown eyes for the first time.

Lana's reaction to Benji's big brown eyes is not so different from a real-life newswoman's, later that day. The reporter happens to sit next to Benji at a picnic lunch. For the first few minutes after the reporter sits down, Benji is busy giving paw-print autographs. But when his fans leave, Benji notices the food on the reporter's plate. He turns to stare at her; she continues eating, trying to ignore him.

Benji moves his face a little closer. He tries to fix her with his big brown eyes. The reporter continues eating. She refuses to look at him. Then Benji comes even closer. He puts a paw on her arm. The reporter peeks at Benji out of the corner of her eye. Their eyes lock, and she gives up. There is no harp music. But it is definitely love. And Benji gets a meatball.

Working with Puppets

AFTER LUNCH, filming begins again. Lana has finished interviewing Benji; and now she, Benji, B.W. (Benji's manager), and Cecil Walker take a tour of Marineland. Benji, of course, is an animal; Lana and B.W. are puppets; Cecil is a person. All of them are supposed to talk to each other as the tour takes place.

For Benji, it's no problem. He's a professional actor. He works with puppets as comfortably as he works with people—or animals—or objects. For the puppets, it's no problem. They'll talk to anyone or anything. But for Cecil, the experience is brand-new.

Cecil Walker with Lana and B. W.

He has never been called upon to talk to puppets before. Cecil is the real-life Assistant General Manager of Marineland. When Joe Camp decided to use Marineland as the setting for Benji's historic dive, Cecil showed Joe around, told him about the dolphins, and introduced him to the many possible settings for the film.

Somehow, it seemed natural to Joe to have Cecil play his real-life role in the television special. And Cecil accepted.

Now Cecil's first scene is taking forever to shoot. Little things keep going wrong. Benji looks in the wrong direction. Cecil talks to the camera instead of to Lana. B.W. slouches.

Over and over they shoot the scene. When the cameras aren't rolling, Lana has to have her hair brushed. B.W. is splashed by the dolphins and has to be blow-dried. Benji needs his steak snacks. Cecil just stands there and doesn't say a word. He's just not used to carrying on conversations with puppets.

Whenever the cameras stop, the puppets talk to each other and to the crew. At one point, Lana turns to Joe. "How come I don't get any treats?" she asks. "Benji does." So Joe feeds her a piece of steak. She coughs. Lana and B.W. try to include Cecil in their conversation, but he just stares into space. He is probably wondering how he ever got himself into this. A responsible executive, taking some puppets and a dog on a tour of Marineland?

But over the next few days, Cecil has other scenes

Benji enjoys everyone's company, but Frank's best of all.

with Lana and B.W. Little by little, Cecil finds it easier to talk to them. They tell him jokes and he laughs. They make wisecracks and he answers back.

After a while, Cecil finds nothing strange about looking into Lana's eyes or whispering to B.W. Grad-

Cecil chats with Lana.

ually, Cecil comes to feel that Lana and B.W. are more than puppets. They have personalities and facial expressions. They make funny remarks and offer opinions. Now, when the cameras stop, Cecil chats with the puppets like everyone else. It's fun and it makes the time go faster.

Benji and the Dolphins

IN THE SCRIPT, Benji is supposed to be immediately fascinated with the dolphins. He's supposed to sneak away from his tour, rush over to the dolphin tank, and look down at the water and bark.

Later on in the script, Benji climbs into the feeding bucket and moves it to the center of the dolphin tank. Then, holding a dead fish in his mouth, he leans over the edge so that the dolphins can see him. A dolphin jumps up and grabs the fish from Benji's mouth.

In Joe's script, there is instant love between Benji and the dolphins. In reality, it didn't quite happen that way.

"The first time he saw a dolphin stick its nose up out of the water," says Frank, "Benji pretty near fell over backwards, he was so scared."

At first, Benji was scared of the dolphins.

It had happened during a scouting trip to Marineland several months before shooting began. "In the beginning," says Frank, "Benji wouldn't even put his feet on the wall. I had to pick him up and put him there. And even then he kept jumping off.

"Well, we just kept doing it until Benji realized that the dolphins were not going to hurt him. After a while, Benji jumped up there himself and walked around.

"Then something happened that ruined all the training. Benji went up in the bucket and held a dead fish in his mouth. A dolphin jumped up nearly fifteen feet to get that fish. Almost knocked Benji's head off. After that, Benji was finished with dolphins . . . dead fish, too."

A dolphin jumped up nearly 15 feet!

MARINELAND
OF FLORIDA

But Frank knew that Benji was going to have to work with the dolphins in the TV special. He was even going to have to go up in the bucket with a dead fish in his mouth.

Frank and Benji went home. Since there were no dolphins in their backyard, there wasn't much Frank could do about lessening Benji's fear of dolphins. But Frank and Benji did work with dead fish.

Frank would put a fish into Benji's mouth and tell him to hold it. Then Frank would ask Benji to do things—with the fish still in his mouth. Benji would walk along a ledge, climb a ladder, jump into the pool, and swim to the side. All the time carrying a fish in his mouth. After a while, a dead fish didn't bother Benji a bit.

Benji learns to stay with the fish.

When they arrived at Marineland to film the TV special, Frank had to teach Benji to like dolphins all over again. Little by little, Benji realized that dolphins are gentle, that when they stick their heads out of the water it is because they are curious, not because they want to hurt him.

After one week, Benji started to hop on the wall just to look at the dolphins. He even learned to let them jump up and take a fish from him. And when he had to jump into the pool with them for the cameras, Benji didn't mind a bit.

In a little more than a week, the real-life Benji was acting like the Benji in the script.

Benji is once more interested in the dolphins.

The Dolphins
and the Shark

IN THE SCRIPT, B. W., Benji's manager, is worried that someone may try to steal Benji's diving gear. B. W. decides to wrap the bubble and jacket in a net bag and drop them into a pool where a ferocious shark can guard them.

"OK," calls Joe. "Let's do the diving gear and shark scene next."

Everyone scurries to the dolphin pool where the scene is to be shot. The art director, who has made a replica of Benji's diving gear to use in this scene, tosses the gear into the pool. But instead of sinking to the bottom, the gear *floats*. Everything is halted until they figure out a way to get the package to sink.

The dolphins who live in the pool have become used to this crazy bunch of people who have been around for the past few weeks. They swim contentedly amidst the chaos.

Once the diving gear is on the bottom of the pool, the next step is to put the shark into the water. They are going to use a realistic-looking, plastic shark.

Two men in diving gear climb into the pool. One is carrying the shark. The other is a camerman carrying an underwater camera. The camerman learned how to do underwater filming when he worked on the movie, *Jaws 2*. He feels very much at home with sharks.

The only problem is that the dolphins do not. They don't know what to make of the shark that has entered their pool. They dart back and forth, bumping the cameraman and stirring up the water so that the scene is nearly impossible to shoot.

The confused dolphins finally calm down, and the filming is completed. Dolphins are very smart animals. They probably figured out that the shark was a phony.

Benji Comes Through Again

THE DAY AFTER the shark scene is filmed, Benji has a scene in which he has to work the controls of the feeding bucket while he rides around above the dolphin pool. When Frank studied the mechanism in the bucket, he decided that working the existing controls would be too difficult for Benji. So the art director constructed a wooden box with special levers to be placed inside the feeder bucket. When the scene of Benji moving the bucket was to be shot, Benji would actually move the levers of the box.

Just before they are ready to shoot the scene, Frank sees the box for the first time. He studies the levers and thinks about the movement that will be required of Benji to pull them. He is concerned. Even these levers are too hard for Benji to pull.

Worried, Frank approaches the art director to discuss the problem. But while Frank is explaining why Benji won't be able to do the job, Benji sits down in front of the box and pulls down one of the levers.

"Well," says Frank. "I'm wrong again."

Benji never fails to get a reward for a job well done.

And Finally . . .

IN THE SCRIPT, Benji spends so much time playing with the dolphins and chasing Boris that he nearly forgets to show up for his dive. The final episode of the TV special shows a very impatient crowd waiting for Benji's arrival. People are beginning to think that the whole thing is a publicity stunt, that Benji doesn't know how to scuba dive after all.

Even Lana, who has very special feelings for Benji, is wondering.

LANA: Just over my shoulder inside this stadium, Benji's manager is attempting to calm

In real life, too, there was a gathering of eager spectators, who grew increasingly impatient.

thousands of impatient spectators. It is becoming increasingly apparent that there will be no dive today.

Then, just as everyone is about to leave, Benji shows up. Cecil steps to the microphone.

CECIL: Ladies and Gentlemen. The moment we've all been waiting for is here. In his diving suit, I present to you the world's first scuba diving dog . . . Benji!

While waiting for a sunny day, Joe angles in on some of the ever-present dolphins.

In real life, too, everyone is beginning to wonder if Benji's dive is ever going to happen. The dive was supposed to have been filmed on Tuesday, but it was postponed. It was postponed on Wednesday. And again on Thursday.

Joe has been waiting for a sunny day. He wants the water to sparkle in the sun as the underwater camera records Benji's dive. There has been no sun for days.

On Friday, during a pouring rain, there is a rumor that a cold front is moving in. Frost is expected on Monday. It begins to look as though Benji is never going to do his scuba diving.

Everyone is uneasy.

• A scuba-diving photographer, who has purchased an underwater camera especially to record Benji's dive, is grumbling that his newspaper wants him on another story.

• Lana, B. W., and Boris keep having to do their scenes one after another, in order to fill up the time Joe has allotted for the dive sequences.

• The underwater cameraman is afraid he may have to leave before he gets to film the dive. He has promised to work for another company on Monday.

Saturday morning starts out like all the other mornings—overcast and dreary. Joe calls for the puppets to report to the beach. It is windy. Lana complains that her hair is blowing all over the place.

Everyone is tired of the terrible weather. But then, just before noon, the sky clears. The sun comes out. The pools sparkle.

"We'll do the dive after lunch," Joe announces.

"Please be careful," Lana is saying.

The excitement begins to bubble through the crew.

"They're putting the dog in!"

"Hey, I don't believe it. He's finally going in."

"OK, Benji, baby. Today's the big day."

Lana seems more concerned than excited. She says to Benji, "It's a very brave thing you are going to do. Please be careful."

"Frank, are you nervous?" asks a reporter.

Frank never looks nervous, but he's always thinking of Benji. Part of his trainer's job is keeping Benji on his toes.

"Well, sure I am. He's done it before at home, but this is a different environment. I don't know how he'll react. Every time's different."

Benji's veterinarian is there. "Doctor, what kind of trouble could there be? What are you worried about?"

"Well, mainly equipment failure. The bubble filling with water or breaking or coming loose."

"Do you have any medical supplies at poolside?"

"Oh, yes. I have an oxygen tank," responds the vet. "But I really don't anticipate any problems. I've never known Benji to panic."

The scene is going to be shot in a pool at the far end of Marineland. As the time gets closer, the area around the pool begins to fill up. In addition to the movie crew, there are Marineland employees, assorted spectators, and five people in wet suits and scuba gear. Richard, Benji's scuba teacher, is going into the pool with the dog. Joe is going underwater to direct the scene, and the cameraman is going to shoot the dive with his underwater camera.

But the most important people in wet suits are the two divers from Marineland. They are carrying rakes

Joe descends underwater to direct the filming.

Richard goes in with Benji.

in their hands, and it is their job to keep away the wildlife that lives in the pool: the giant four-foot turtles, the barracuda, the small sharks, the groupers, and a sawfish. Some of those creatures could swallow Benji in one gulp.

"Now remember," Joe warns the divers as they enter the water, "nothing, but nothing gets close to Benji."

Benji's wire platforms are already in the water. They are the same ones that Benji used in his backyard pool. Benji will be placed on one of them. Then both platforms will be lowered to a level of six feet under water. Benji will swim from one to the other, ten feet away.

Benji is suited up and attached to his air hose.

Benji is suited up and safely attached to his air hose. He is lifted onto the platform by Richard. Frank is standing above the pool holding his underwater microphone. The vet is standing next to Frank.

Richard makes a final check of Benji's equipment and signals for the platforms to be lowered. Inch by inch Benji descends until he is six feet below.

Suddenly a small shark swims near Benji. The divers don't see it. Only the people out of the pool watch nervously as the shark swims past Benji.

"OK, Benji," calls Frank into his microphone. "Swim, Benji, come on. Swim. Swim."

Benji pushes himself off the platform.

"Good. Now swim, Benji. Swim. Come on, Benji, swim."

Benji's legs begin to move. His feet dance and paddle through the water.

It is an incredible scene: Benji, in his bubble and his blue and red jacket, is six feet under water— swimming like a fish, sharing a pool with sharks and turtles, with tropical fish and a barracuda.

As Benji paddles, his colorful, graceful shape slips smoothly through the water, his trail marked by bubbles.

Perhaps, as he paddles, Benji is observing Joe and the camerman and the Marineland divers who are with him under the water. Or perhaps he is watching the tropical fish that are swimming nearby. Perhaps Benji is wondering why he has never seen such strange but beautiful animals before.

No one will ever know what Benji is looking at while he swims. But it is obvious that Benji is happy as he wiggles his way through the water, his fur flowing, his legs paddling, his tiny body sleek in its diving suit.

Finally, after an hour of scuba diving, Benji emerges to cheers and applause. Applause born of amazement: Benji has done what many thought was impossible. Applause born of relief: Benji is safe.

Once Benji is out of his suit, he is tail-wagging happy. He loves the attention, the petting, the praise, the steak. As he swallows his reward, Benji stands calmly and proudly; Frank is using a blow dryer to dry Benji's fur.

Meanwhile, just as proud, but minus a wagging tail, Joe Camp climbs out of the pool. A year ago, he had had a crazy idea. Today, Benji proved that it wasn't so crazy after all.

Benji receives congratulations.

MARINELAND OF FLORIDA